31 Days of Prayer

Repent, for the kingdom of heaven is near

Mark Anderson Smith

Copyright

Dedication

For Teri, my wife,
who inspired me to do better, to be better,
and who taught me, more than anyone,
that God forgives

Other books by this author:

31 Days of Prayer series
The Commands of Jesus

Fiction
The Great Scottish Land Grab
Fallen Warriors

Non-Fiction
Double Your Salary …without losing your
soul!

~~~~~~~~~~~~~~~~~~~~~~~~~~~~~

Introduction

~~~~~~~~~~~~~~~~~~~~~~~~~~~~~

...the kindness of God leads you to
repentance...
Romans 2 v 4 (NASB)

Repent, for the kingdom of heaven is near...
This is how Jesus begins to teach, a simple
instruction with a combination of promise and
warning. How do you feel when you read or
hear the word: repent? For most of my life
I've had a negative reaction to the term,
associating repentance with guilt and shame.
Yet I value repentance since it was the catalyst
for me to finally believe I was part of the
kingdom of heaven.

My first major experience of repentance
was of arriving at the understanding that God
loved me, that he loved me to such an extent
that he was willing to pay the penalty for my
sin through Jesus on the cross. Faced with this
realisation, I knew that I could not simply
continue to act as I had before. A change was
required. Looking back at that experience I
can see now that I was surrounded by the

kindness of God. Before, while I was struggling against God, he was calling me to him. He was already at work in my life, helping me to understand my need for him. Of course, long before, Jesus had died in my place. That was a done deal, God telling the whole world that there was nothing standing in the way of our returning to him. Then afterwards, for the first time in my life I knew I was part of the kingdom of heaven. I was loved, I was valued. I always had been and yet never realised how much. You are valued and loved just as much as I ever was.

It is my hope as you pray and study Jesus teaching on repentance and the kingdom of heaven with me, that you will know and be able to accept the kindness of God towards you.

Yours in Christ

Mark Anderson Smith

*"And forgive us our debts,
as we also have forgiven our debtors.
And lead us not into temptation,
but deliver us from the evil one."
Matthew 6 v 12 to 13*

I've struggled with feelings of guilt many times. Something I've noticed is that those feelings of guilt often keep me from turning back to God. I feel ashamed and this discourages me from praying. I know that God is merciful, that he forgives, yet I have this mental blockage hindering my desire to receive his forgiveness and be free from guilt and shame.

The Lord's prayer, recorded in Matthew 6, is an amazing tool for overcoming guilt and shame. Look at how Jesus laid it out:

*"This, then, is how you should pray:
"'Our Father in heaven,
hallowed be your name,"*

First Jesus tells us to praise our father in heaven. No matter what we've done, or how badly we feel about ourselves, Jesus tells us we can praise and worship God. I do often find that the act of choosing to praise God, either telling him or singing to him, changes my perspective on life.

"Your kingdom come.
Your will be done, on earth as it is in
heaven."

Then Jesus tells us to seek God's will and his kingdom here on earth. This is such a broad statement. What is God's will? What does it mean for God's kingdom to come on earth? However, we're guided by the condition: "as it is in heaven". We are to ask God to influence and affect and change our lives, the lives of our family, our neighbours, our colleagues, such that God's kingdom is displayed and victorious. We are not to pray that our will be done, no! God's will. God's kingdom. This requires us to try and understand what God's will is, what God's kingdom is like. And it is a challenge as we discover this, to live our own lives in accordance with God's will and his kingdom.

"Give us today our daily bread."

Always practical, Jesus tells us to ask God to provide for our needs. Again, no matter how badly we feel about ourselves, Jesus tells us to ask God to provide for us. If we can humble ourselves to ask God, perhaps there will be times when we can humble ourselves to ask others for help as well. And God will provide. Perhaps not all that you have asked for, or what you were expecting, but certainly everything you really need.

"And forgive us our debts, as we also have forgiven our debtors."

I love this interpretation of Jesus words. I've seen them interpreted as forgive our trespasses. Debts… Trespasses… Two different words to describe another word that is sometimes used: sin. Forgive us…

Forgive us, yes, but note the position here. Only after we've praised you, only after we've asked you to extend your kingdom here on earth, only after we've asked you to provide for us…

Praise God that he welcomes us despite our sin, despite our weakness, listens to us, hears us, responds to us. Be assured, there is nothing in your life so horrendous that God will not hear you when you call to him.

"And lead us not into temptation, but deliver us from the evil one.'"

Finally, Jesus tells us to seek God's guidance. That we might not walk towards temptation, that we will be delivered from evil. If we are to be serious about repentance, we need God's help to warn us. There will be areas of our lives where sin is obvious, but even then we can risk everything by flirting with danger.

I could focus on how playing with fire might lead us not just to get burned, but consumed, or worse, burn others, but I want to flip this around. This is Jesus final instruction on how to pray. God's desire for us is that he be allowed to lead us on a path that will ensure us eternal life. If the opposite of evil is good, then to be delivered from evil is to be allowed to live a good life.

A good life... Would you like to live a good life? That is God's desire for you. Will you let him lead you into a good life?

Our father in heaven, teach us how to pray. Give us a vision of what good life you have planned for us. May we seek to learn from you what it means for your kingdom to reign in our lives and our community, and may we desire to bring this into being. Help us to accept and believe that you are always waiting to hear us, and that you will never turn us away. Amen.

***…the kindness of God
leads you to repentance
Romans 2 v 4 (NASB)***

I love this statement by Paul, that it's God's kindness that leads us towards repentance. Some people have a picture of God as a tyrant, sitting in judgement, always watching for what we do wrong. When I read God's word, I get a very different sense. A father who longs to be at peace with his children, someone who is patient far beyond my own breaking point, a king who has been wronged, yet is willing to forgive.

The statement above by Paul has been a great comfort to me. While our creator has in the past shown he is more than capable of punishing, there is ample evidence to show that God has no desire to. As any good parent desires, he wants to warn his children from danger and teach them to do what is right, before they get hurt.

There are consequences in this life for what we do. If we will admit it, certain actions can hurt others and hurt ourselves. The original ten commandments contained a number of universal principles that are commonly adopted into law around the world. Murdering people is always seen as wrong. Stealing likewise. While cultures in the Western world have attempted to dismiss the crime of adultery, anyone who has been betrayed by a spouse knows the pain that causes. Has anyone ever lied about you to damage your reputation? How did that make you feel, or how would it make you feel?

It is the kindness of God that warns us that our actions will have consequences, kindness that pleads with us to choose a different path, kindness that does not want us to hurt others or ourselves.

And there are consequences for ourselves, both in this life and in the life to come. Guilt and shame are two immediate consequences. How many have suffered whole lives plagued by guilt and shame? There may be other consequences: injury, incarceration, loss of job, loss of family, of friends.

But in the end we are offered two destinations: life or death. The God who created us wants us to choose life. We may not have had much of a life up to this point, but Jesus came, he said, that you might have life to the full! Not just now, but in eternity.

And this is the ultimate kindness of God: that despite our past, he chooses to offer us the possibility of repentance, to turn to him and be accepted into his kingdom.

Our father in heaven, thank you for your kindness towards us, to me. May I turn from those actions which have hurt others, have hurt myself, and which have disappointed you. I choose to repent. Help me to understand what that means and to follow you. Amen.

Day 3   Forgive as we have been forgiven

*Then Peter came to Jesus and asked,
"Lord, how many times shall I
forgive my brother or sister
who sins against me? Up to seven times?"
Jesus answered,
"I tell you, not seven times,
but seventy-seven times."
Matthew 18 v 21 to 22*

Some people find it easier to forgive than others. Personally I find it quite hard to forgive. I sometimes take far longer than I should to let go of hurt or pain and anger. Yet even as I drag forgiveness out, I'm conscious of Jesus answer to Peter, that it is not enough to forgive seven times, but seventy-seven times… Some translations say seventy times seven, but this seems to be one of several occasions where Jesus was not so concerned with the specifics, but was wanting to hammer home a point: We should never stop forgiving those who sin against us.

And if this wasn't clear, Jesus goes on to

share a story about a servant whose debt is forgiven by the master, but then who will not forgive the debt another servant owes to them. The master is told and...

"Then the master called the servant in. 'You wicked servant,' he said, 'I cancelled all that debt of yours because you begged me to. Shouldn't you have had mercy on your fellow servant just as I had on you?' In anger his master handed him over to the jailers to be tortured, until he should pay back all he owed. "This is how my heavenly Father will treat each of you unless you forgive your brother or sister from your heart."
Matthew 18 v 32 to 35

What an ending! What a warning! We are to forgive those who sin against us as God forgives us: completely, mercifully, totally. If we do not, then we risk having our merciful God turn against us.

"And forgive us our debts, as we also have forgiven our debtors."
Matthew 6 v 12

You will remember this verse from Day 1. Forgive us... as we also have forgiven. Even in this most merciful and gracious of prayers, Jesus placed a condition that we are to live by. A warning that we should heed. If we will not forgive those who sin against us, how can we expect the Lord God, King of heaven, to forgive us? The kingdom of heaven is not a weak place, somewhere we can take for granted. There's an expectation on us that the kindness we receive will be passed onto others. And so the kingdom grows, as those who receive mercy show mercy to those who also do not deserve it.

Our father in heaven, remind us of how much you have forgiven us, and help us to see those who hurt or sin against us with a heart of forgiveness and mercy and kindness. May we show the same kindness and mercy to others as you showed to us. Amen.

Day 4 The Lord waits for you

"In repentance and rest you will be saved,
In quietness and trust is your strength."
But you were not willing...
Isaiah 30 v 15 (NASB)

Repentance and rest are two concepts I struggle to place together, yet as I read the verse above, I find this a comfort. Isaiah is challenging the people of Israel to return to their God, and how should they return? Through repentance *and* rest, in quietness *and* trust.

When I think about repentance, I often have a picture in my mind of kneeling down, wearing sackcloth, being covered in ashes. In my imagination it seems to require a great effort. Isaiah corrects that picture and transforms it to one of sitting or even lying next to God as a child might relax next to their father.

But you were not willing... What a rebuke! To be offered the easy way out, salvation, your strength renewed, and to have rejected that offer. I encourage you to read the rest of the passage, from Isaiah 30 verse 15 through to verse 26. Those in Israel who rejected the comfort of God, who chose to flee from the enemies who surrounded them, would be granted their wish! Fear, loss, and isolation would be their curse instead of the blessing God offered.

However all is not lost for you. Just as Isaiah's warning to Israel was an opportunity for them to return to the God of rest, quietness and trust. Isaiah goes on to make this promise:

> *Therefore the Lord longs*
> *to be gracious to you,*
> *And therefore He waits on high*
> *to have compassion on you.*
> *For the Lord is a God of justice;*
> *How blessed are all those*
> *who long for Him.*
> *Isaiah 30 v 18 (NASB)*

Have you ever considered that the Lord is longing to be gracious to you? That God waits to have compassion on you?

But why would God wait you may ask? He

wants us to long for him. As you continue to read through the passage, we find that God is waiting for the sound of our cry to him. He is also waiting for us to "desecrate" the idols we worship in our lives, to "scatter" them far from us and choose to tell these idols to "Be gone!"

When Jesus was asked what the greatest commandment was, he did not immediately say to love our neighbour as ourselves. No, instead he answered:

"You shall love the Lord your God with all your heart, and with all your soul, and with all your mind."
Matthew 22 v 37 (NASB)

What is there in our lives that we love with our heart, with our soul, with our mind? Our God is looking for us to love him first, foremost, with passion, with determination, with intent.

And the promise he gives to those of us who will do this is rest, quietness, trust, and also to provide for our needs. At that time: rain for the seed sown in the ground, a rich and plentiful harvest, a wide pasture, light to guide our way, and healing of all wounds.

Some of these will always be relevant, others I believe are symbolic of a bountiful provision.

The Lord is waiting for you. What are you waiting for?

Our father in heaven, may we wait no longer. May we turn to you in repentance and rest, trusting in you for your forgiveness, for your peace, for your provision. May you help us to choose to love you, with all our heart, with all our soul, with all our mind and discard from our lives anything that keeps us from doing this. Amen.

Day 5   Do you show contempt?

*…do you show contempt
for the riches of his kindness,
forbearance and patience,
not realising that God's kindness
is intended to lead you to repentance?
Romans 2 v 4*

Imagine the situation… You receive a phone call telling you your brother has been shot. He's been taken to hospital. You rush down there but it's too late. He's dead. Then the details start to come out. Your brother was home. Someone walked into his apartment, a police officer, and for no good reason shot him. How would you feel? Angry? Confused?

I would want justice. I would want that officer arrested and punished.

In September 2018 Dallas police officer Amber Guyger walked into the apartment of her neighbour, Botham Jean, allegedly thinking it was her own apartment and shot him. Initially Guyger was charged with manslaughter, but later she was charged and ultimately found guilty of murder. Botham Jean's brother, Brandt, was at the sentencing hearing and was allowed to give a statement.

"I forgive you, and I know if you go to God and ask him, he will forgive you... I love you just like anyone else... I personally want the best for you... I don't even want you to go to jail. I want the best for you because I know that's what Botham would want you to do, and the best would be give your life to Christ."

And then Brandt asks the judge if he can give the killer of his brother a hug. It is a remarkable illustration of kindness and a call to repentance.

I started these 31 days pointing out that God's kindness is intended to lead us to repentance. But context is very important. In Paul's letter to the Romans, he has just called them out for hypocritical judgement. While there is a time and a place to judge, as Jesus said: we need to deal with the plank in our own eye before trying to "help" others. Paul's statement on kindness is part of the question above. His answer is devastating:

But because of your stubbornness and your unrepentant heart, you are storing up wrath against yourself for the day of God's

wrath, when his righteous judgement will be revealed. God "will repay each person according to what they have done." To those who by persistence in doing good seek glory, honour and immortality, he will give eternal life. But for those who are self-seeking and who reject the truth and follow evil, there will be wrath and anger.
Romans 2 v 5 to 8

In some ways, this is just brutal. To anyone who is self-seeking, who rejects the truth and follows evil, there will be wrath and anger. That picture some have of God as tyrant, well, God's word warns there will be a day of judgement. For some that will be a brutal day. There will be no mercy. No forgiveness. No offers of a hug or kind words.

Yet it doesn't have to be that way. Kindness, forbearance, and patience--these are what God offers us now, a chance to repent, to turn back to him. Each of us is offered the same chance. We are shown what is expected of us, how to turn our life around. To those who by persistence in doing good seek glory, honour and immortality, he will give eternal life.

Our Father in Heaven, thank you for your great patience and your kindness. Show us what is evil in our lives, and may we turn from that, cease to only seek to please ourselves, and accept your truth. May we not despise your patience or kindness, but instead commit ourselves to seeking your glory, your honour and immortality through Jesus your son. Amen.

Day 6   The hope God offers

*"For God so loved the world
that he gave his one and only Son,
that whoever believes in him
shall not perish but have eternal life."*
John 3 v 16

God's call for us to repent gives us hope! In today's culture there seems to be a very vocal minority who take pleasure in destroying lives. Calling for people to be fired from their job, for them to be banned from public speaking, prevented from making a living, or even from communicating with others. There seems little willingness to forgive, no desire to rehabilitate, and no consideration that a different perspective may have equal or greater weight. Once offended, some will stop at nothing to crush those who have dared speak out of turn.

Our creator God has far more right than any other to hold us to account. He created this world, he established the rules of the game, and he has the ability to judge and punish as he sees fit. But instead of damning us all to hell when we reject his rules, he offers us the ultimate get out of jail card!

I will keep coming back to this most beautiful of Jesus statements: "For God so loved the world, that he sent his one and only son, that whosoever believes, shall not perish, but have everlasting life."

If you do not currently believe: repent of your unbelief, choose to believe in Jesus, and you are promised you will have eternal life.

What a contrast to those today who seek to silence and destroy! Yes, God does challenge us. Does hold us to account for what we have done and said, but his desire is not to destroy us, but instead to save us.

Jesus statement above is arguably his most well known. However it is well worth reading what he went on to say:

"For God did not send his Son into the world to condemn the world, but to save the world through him. Whoever believes in him is not condemned, but whoever does not believe stands condemned already because they have not believed in the name of God's one and only Son. This is the verdict: Light has come into the world, but people loved darkness instead

of light because their deeds were evil.
Everyone who does evil hates the light,
and will not come into the light for fear
that their deeds will be exposed. But
whoever lives by the truth comes into the
light, so that it may be seen plainly that
what they have done has been done in the
sight of God."
John 3 v 17 to 21

God's desire is for us to be saved through Jesus. The implication is that we need saving. That we have already been judged and found guilty. We stand condemned if we have not believed in the name of God's one and only son. I imagine that for some, these may not be easy words to hear. To be challenged that your deeds are evil, that you have loved darkness rather than light for this very reason. Know this: Your creator has the right to judge you. The one who gave you life has the right to hold you to account. He desires to give you life, to forgive all, to call you his child. There is a cost to all this. The greatest cost. Jesus life, given in your place. There is another cost, your willingness to repent, to turn from anything in your life that is dark to God's light. To open up your life to him.

God's promise to you is that if you do this, he will be faithful and he will forgive.

Our father in heaven, thank you for Jesus, for his message that you love us, that your desire for us is to have eternal life with you. Thank you for Jesus sacrifice, for his willingness to die in our place so that we need not perish. May we bring all our deeds into your light, and let you guide us in how we should live. Amen.

Day 7   Weeping and gnashing of teeth

"But suppose that servant is wicked and says to himself, 'My master is staying away a long time,' and he then begins to beat his fellow servants and to eat and drink with drunkards. The master of that servant will come on a day when he does not expect him and at an hour he is not aware of. He will cut him to pieces and assign him a place with the hypocrites, where there will be weeping and gnashing of teeth."
Matthew 24 v 48 to 51

The kingdom of heaven is near, yet almost 2,000 years after Jesus warned us to repent, we are still waiting for his return. Jesus must have known that we would need to wait and impressed on his disciples several stories to force the point. It is not enough to repent for a time, we need to be on our guard, alert and always expecting Jesus return. There are eternal consequences for our actions, and assuming that what we do will not matter risks us descending to our worst behaviour.

Following Jesus warning of the consequences for those who are not faithful or wise, he goes on to tell three stories, each reinforcing his warning. Three stories which each describe a facet of the kingdom of heaven...

Firstly a contrast is made between five foolish bridesmaids and five wise ones. The foolish ones were unprepared for a long wait and did not take extra oil for their lamps. The wise bridesmaids thought ahead and brought extra oil. Interestingly, all fell asleep while waiting for the bridegroom. When the bridegroom arrived, the wise bridesmaids were able to refill their lamps and head off to the wedding feast. The foolish bridesmaids tried to buy oil, but it was too late, they were shut out of the wedding feast.

I'm struck by Jesus saying this is a picture of the kingdom of heaven "at that time" when he is about to return. Both the wise and the foolish are present in the kingdom of heaven. Will we be ready for his return, or be shown to have been foolish?

Then the kingdom of heaven is described as a man entrusting his money to his servants while he went away. Some servants invested and used his money to generate an income and so were rewarded, while one servant incurs the man's wrath by doing nothing, and having the gall to insult the man on his return. This last servant is described as lazy and wicked. Lazy as he made no effort to work for his master, wicked because he did this despite claiming to know his master was a hard man who took what did not belong to him. Just as some bridesmaids received the reward for their preparedness, the wise servants also are given a reward. The punishment of the wicked servant uses the same language as above, everything he has is to be taken from him and he is to be thrown outside "where there will be weeping and gnashing of teeth."

The last story is known as The Sheep and the Goats. We are the sheep and the goats. We will be separated. The sheep will be told:

"I was hungry and you gave me something to eat, I was thirsty and you gave me something to drink, I was a stranger and you invited me in, I needed clothes and you clothed me, I was sick and you looked after me, I was in prison and you came to visit me."
Matthew 25 v 35 to 36

Simple practical ways of caring for those in need. It doesn't take a lot to do what is right.

But the goats do none of these things and again there is a warning of punishment, this time being cast into the eternal fire which has been prepared for the devil and his angels.

When Jesus taught his disciples, the kingdom of heaven was near, but for us today the kingdom of heaven is now. It is the choices we make, our actions, our decisions. For these there will be consequences, good or bad. Choose wisely!

Our father in heaven, help us to understand that we are living in the kingdom of heaven, that everything we do has an eternal consequence. May we act with this knowledge and seek to live wisely, with kindness and mercy and compassion. Amen

Flee the evil desires of youth and pursue righteousness, faith, love and peace, along with those who call on the Lord out of a pure heart.
2 Timothy 2 v 22

It is not enough to stop doing something. Repentance must result in a change of direction. If you stop, you are still where you were, temptation and sin within grasp.

In the book of Genesis, we're told Joseph's story. Sold into slavery by jealous brothers, he gained the respect and trust of his owner, Potiphar, who placed him in charge of the household. Potiphar's wife began to take notice of Joseph and attempted to seduce him. Joseph's response shows his character:

"My master has withheld nothing from me except you, because you are his wife. How then could I do such a wicked thing and sin against God?"
Genesis 39 v 9

But no matter how much responsibility Joseph had been given, he was a slave. He had no rights. Potiphar's wife didn't take no for an answer and kept trying to seduce him. Joseph could not hand in his notice, could not even raise a complaint. Yet when Potiphar's wife tried to trap him, insisting he go to bed with her, Joseph fled from the house.

For that moral stance, Potiphar's wife took her revenge and Joseph was put in prison. Not the outcome I expect Joseph would have wanted. Did he wonder if he had made a mistake, if it would have been better for him to give in? Fortunately for us all, he did not. Joseph continued to seek God, continued to have faith in God even though he was in prison for at least two years, probably much longer. After some time we're told that Joseph interpreted the dreams of two other prisoners, correctly prophesying that one would be saved and the other executed. This led to Joseph eventually being called to interpret Pharaoh's dream and saving not just the country of Egypt from famine, but also the new nation of Israel.

Throughout his life, Joseph chose to pursue righteousness, defending his master's honour, working to save people from the famine.

Would he have been given such responsibility if he had given into sin?

Are there evil desires in your life that you should flee from? Remember that it is not enough to turn away from those evil desires, you must turn to something, to someone. Turn to Jesus who offers you comfort, peace, joy, and a full life.

Our father in heaven, where there is temptation in our life, give us the wisdom to flee from it and turn to you. Help us to seek your righteousness, your faith, your love and your peace. Amen.

"…when they turn back to you and give praise to your name, praying… then hear from heaven and forgive the sin of your people Israel…"
1 Kings 8 v 33 to 34

Known for his wisdom, Solomon built a temple to God as one of his first acts as king. He dedicated the temple with a series of prayers, several of which acknowledged the possibility, or even probability, that the nation of Israel would need to repent.

"When anyone wrongs their neighbour…"
"When your people Israel have been defeated by an enemy because they have sinned against you…"
"When the heavens are shut up and there is no rain because your people have sinned against you…"
"When famine or plague comes to the land… whatever disaster or disease may come…"
1 Kings 8 v 31 to 37

Centuries before, Moses warned Israel of consequences for turning away from God. These were laid out in the promise of curses that would befall the nation. Reading through this list of curses in Deuteronomy 28 it is striking how many could be applied to the UK today. Each curse not just a punishment, but an indication of how far they had turned from God, a more severe withdrawal of blessing that might wake Israel up and finally bring them to their senses. God's hope was that Israel would not remain estranged from him but return in repentance.

While the curses warned of by Moses and the prayers of Solomon were given for the nation of Israel, even in Solomon's prayers he indicated that both God's judgement and God's mercy are not just for a whole nation, but for us as individuals. If our lives are being affected by disasters we have the right to lift up our hands to God, to ask him to hear us, to forgive us. Yet Solomon did not just ask God for forgiveness, but for God to treat us as we deserve, according to all we do:

"...deal with each man according to all he does, since you know his heart..."
1 Kings 8 v 39

Stop and consider this... Do you really want God to treat you the way you deserve, to curse us for all and any evil we have done?

It is not God's desire to curse us, that is why there are so many warnings throughout God's word. Like any good father, he wants us to know what is dangerous and how to avoid it. And when we have failed, fallen, slipped up, sinned, God still does not want to curse us, but wants us to confess, to turn back to him, and he wants to forgive, to heal, to restore our lives. Thanks be to God that we can call on his mercy, call on his kindness, and choose ourselves to turn away from sin and towards him.

Our father in heaven, may I turn away from sin and towards you. May I choose to praise you, to humble myself before you, to lift up my hands to you and seek you. Forgive my sin, have mercy on me even though I do not deserve it. Teach me how to live, deliver me from disaster and provide for my needs. Amen.

If we claim to be without sin, we deceive ourselves and the truth is not in us. If we confess our sins, he is faithful and just and will forgive us our sins and purify us from all unrighteousness. If we claim we have not sinned, we make him out to be a liar and his word is not in us.
1 John 1 v 8 to 10

For the last fifteen years I've worked in part as a software programmer. When I read John's statement, I recognise a similarity between this and a standard programming statement:

IF a fact is true, THEN something must happen. ELSE, since the fact is not true, then something different must happen.

If... Then... Else statements are commonly used by programmers to manage and direct what happens when code is run. These statements can be extremely complex, yet they can always be broken down into relatively simple components. In this case: If the first part of the statement is true, the next part happens. If the first part is not true, or to put it another way: is false, then the second part happens.

God's word is full of relatively simple If... Then... Else... statements and the quote above from John's letter is a great example. Let's break it down.

If we claim either that we are without sin, or that we have not sinned Then:

- We are lying to ourselves
- The truth, that is Jesus, is not in us
- We are calling God a liar
- God's word—Jesus—is not in us

Else, if we confess our sins Then:

- God is faithful to his promise to forgive
- God is just—he will ensure justice is done—however, not what we deserve, but instead, Jesus will take any punishment on our behalf
- Our sins will be forgiven
- We will be purified from all unrighteousness

John uses multiple If statements and it is not enough to just meet one condition: to tell the truth. To acknowledge our sin we also have to meet the second condition: to actually confess our sin.

Our first responsibility is to confess to God. He already knows of course, but it does us good to verbally acknowledge our sin.

Catholics have a long tradition of confession to a priest. Alcoholics Anonymous have helped millions worldwide to find a way to confess a particular sin in a setting that echoes the promise John shares above. If confessing to family or friends or others, you are not asking them to keep a secret. Confessing to others requires us to humble ourselves, to reveal our sin and bring it into the light. It may be scary or even terrifying yet can often help to break the hold that sin has over us.

But what of those we have sinned against? The twelve steps of AA include this wisdom:

[We will make] direct amends to [people we have harmed] wherever possible, except when to do so would injure them or others.

If you are in any doubt whether you might

further injure someone you have sinned
against, it would be wise to seek advice.

One final caveat. While Jesus takes on the
punishment that otherwise God would
allocate to us, Man's law may allocate a
different punishment for certain sins. If we
have ignored the warnings in God's word
about breaking Man's law, then God does not
promise us a get out of jail free card.
However, even those who are found guilty in
Man's court, can find freedom and release in
their heart and spirit and mind, when they
have confessed to God and received his
forgiveness.

*Our father in heaven, help us to
acknowledge the truth about sin in our
lives. May we confess to you that we have
sinned and allow you to shine your
cleansing light into our hearts and minds,
to expose sin that we may not even be
aware of. May we believe your promise
that you are faithful and just and that you
will forgive us when we confess our sin to
you. Give us courage to confess to others
when appropriate, and face up to the
consequences of our actions. Amen.*

Is anyone among you in trouble? Let them pray. Is anyone happy? Let them sing songs of praise. Is anyone among you sick? Let them call the elders of the church to pray over them and anoint them with oil in the name of the Lord. And the prayer offered in faith will make the sick person well; the Lord will raise them up. If they have sinned, they will be forgiven. Therefore confess your sins to each other and pray for each other so that you may be healed. The prayer of a righteous person is powerful and effective.
James 5 v 13 to 16

What an ending to James' letter to the early church!

- If you are in trouble - pray.
- If you are happy - sing songs of praise.
- Are you sick - call on the elders of the church to pray over you and anoint you with oil.

There is a promise with that last instruction, that if the sick person does this, the prayer offered in faith will make them well - "the Lord will raise them up."

This promise is followed by another: if the sick person has sinned, they will be forgiven. Yet this promise is also followed by another instruction: "Therefore confess your sins to each other and pray for each other so that you may be healed."

It's not complicated and we shouldn't try to read more into this than is there. James is not saying all sick people have sinned, he is saying that key word: if... Yet the fact he mentions confessing sin means we should take note of this. If there is unconfessed sin in our lives we should confess this. And where we are sick we should ask others, especially those who are stronger in their faith, to pray for us.

Are any of us righteous? It seems that many people have a hang up on the word. Yet right back at the beginning the term is defined as a simple childlike faith:

"Abram believed the Lord, and he credited it to him as righteousness."
Genesis 15 v 6

Believing God, that is what makes us righteous. And those who believe God, who believe in God's promises, who believe that God answers their prayers... The prayers of those people are powerful and effective!

Jesus made the point several times that only those who received the kingdom of heaven like a little child would enter it. It seems that our journey in Christ is to learn how to receive and accept the promises of God, trusting him, believing him, being obedient to him. Will you take the hand of your father in heaven today and allow him to lead you?

Our father in heaven, thank you that you hear us when we are in trouble and turn to you. Thank you that you want to share in our joy when we are happy. Thank you that you care about us when we are sick and want to heal us. Thank you that you do not want us to be burdened by sin and guilt, but encourage us to be free of it. Thank you and praise you that you have made simple trust in you such a powerful and effective force for good in this world! Amen.

Day 12   Sackcloth and Ashes

"…if the miracles that were performed in you had been performed in Tyre and Sidon, they would have repented long ago, sitting in sackcloth and ashes."
Luke 10 verse 13

Sometimes confession of sin just isn't enough. We know it deep in our hearts. We've gone too far, done too much, for too long.

Jesus called out two towns in the passage the above verse is taken from, Chorazin and Bethsaida. Having revealed himself as the son of God, demonstrating his power through miracles, the people of these towns still did not repent. Contrast this with the experience of Jonah who was told to prophesy destruction on the city of Nineveh:

Jonah obeyed the word of the Lord and went to Nineveh. Now Nineveh was a very large city; it took three days to go through it. Jonah began by going a day's journey into the city, proclaiming, "Forty more

**days and Nineveh will be overthrown."
The Ninevites believed God. A fast was
proclaimed, and all of them, from the
greatest to the least, put on sackcloth.
Jonah 3 v 3 to 5**

We're not told in Jonah the entirety of why Nineveh was to be overthrown, other than for wickedness and violence, but the people knew, and their response was to fast and stop wearing fine clothes and instead wear sackcloth.

I've never worn sackcloth, but I understand it to be coarse, scratchy, and uncomfortable. It would not have been pleasant to wear, but a constant reminder of the threat of destruction. Wearing scratchy clothing, their stomachs growling for lack of food, these people demonstrated they had heard the message God had sent, they turned from their wickedness and God relented and spared them.

I do not have a message of God for the UK, but I look and listen and wonder how far we are as a country from God. Writing this in the middle of a pandemic that mirrors a biblical plague. What was our response as a country? Oh yes, we clapped for the NHS…

Do we need to repent as a country? Do you need to repent, do I…?

Repentance is a turning away from sin and towards God. It can help us to show our repentance through giving up or accepting a form of suffering. Of course, Jesus said that we should not tell or reveal when we fast, but he was talking about acts of righteousness, not acts of repentance.

I've experimented with fasting while writing this. I've had some failures… I've found that I can fast from breakfast and lunch, one day a week, without it impacting on my work. I probably overdid things when I attempted to give up sugar, and food and drink containing sugar, completely for 31 days. My wife told me a few days later that the reason I felt like I was having an emotional breakdown was because my body was still trying to adjust after the cold turkey way I'd stopped consuming sugar. After a couple of weeks the highs and lows I was experiencing settled down and then it was just a daily reminder that I'd chosen to avoid sugar.

The singer Johnny Cash chose to wear black for much of his life and his song: The Man in Black makes the claim this was to bring to his mind the poor, the oppressed, prisoners and those who've never heard the words of Jesus.

I've not read anywhere of a call to repentance also including instructions about how people should debase themselves. It seems that we know instinctively there are things we should do, or give up, or change as a sign to ourselves, and sometimes to others, and always to God, that we've understood, we've listened, that we are taking repentance seriously.

Our father in heaven, where we need to repent as individuals, as a country, help us to humble ourselves and repent. To turn from wickedness, whatever its form, and turn to you. Where it will be helpful to us to mark our repentance, guide us and lead us. Keep us from making vows that we cannot keep, from changing things that will hurt us or others. But as Jesus suffered for us, may we not be afraid to embrace discomfort and hunger to show our repentance. Amen.

'Why have we fasted,' they say,
'and you have not seen it?
Why have we humbled ourselves,
and you have not noticed?'
"Yet on the day of your fasting,
you do as you please
and exploit all your workers.
Your fasting ends in quarrelling and strife,
and in striking each other
with wicked fists.
You cannot fast as you do today
and expect your voice to be heard on high.
Isaiah 58 v 3 to 4

I am no expert in fasting. I've had some experiences that I'm ashamed of. As a teenager I fasted for two days, and then gorged myself almost sick when I started eating again. I have never fasted for a longer period. Instead I've fasted infrequently, sometimes with many years between attempts. One of my most successful occasions was a week I tried what I called a Daniel fast, only eating fruit and vegetables, abstaining from meat, from anything processed, and alcohol. At the end of that week I did fast a whole day and found I had strength to work normally.

As I wrote earlier, while writing this book I've attempted to fast on a more regular basis. This was actually a continuation of a fast at the urging of my pastor who called on the church to fast every Wednesday, all who were able during the first months of the pandemic. I tried fasting a whole day, from after an evening meal, not eating until the second day when I had breakfast. I found this affected my work so cut back.

As Isaiah wrote above, we should not expect God to pay attention to our fasting if our lives do not change, and especially if they get worse! If you cannot cope without regular meals, finding your temper flares, or the way you treat people suffers, then it would be better to avoid fasting from food.

Yet as I wrote previously, there is benefit in doing something to show we are humbling ourselves before God, and for those who can fast, this can be a useful method to expose our hearts.

Regardless of whether we choose to not eat, or do something else to humble ourselves before God, Isaiah goes on to share a series of actions that all of us can do to show we want to be obedient to God:

Is not this the kind of fasting
I have chosen:
to loose the chains of injustice...
to set the oppressed free...
Is it not to share your food with the hungry
and to provide the poor wanderer
with shelter--
when you see the naked, to clothe them,
and not to turn away from your own flesh
and blood? Isaiah 58 v 6 to 7

And for those who do this there is a promise:

Then you will call,
and the Lord will answer;
you will cry for help,
and he will say: Here am I.
Isaiah 58 v 9

And there is more... Note the If... Then... contract that God offers us:

If you do away with the
yoke of oppression,
with the pointing finger
and malicious talk,
and if you spend yourselves
in behalf of the hungry
and satisfy the needs of the oppressed,
then your light will rise in the darkness,
and your night will become
like the noonday.
The Lord will guide you always;
he will satisfy your needs...
Isaiah 58 v 9 to 11

All of us can make an effort to not be people who oppress others. A pointing finger, malicious talk, forms of bullying found from the dining table to the school yard to neighbourhoods and places of work everywhere.

If I'm in any doubt of my ability to "spend" myself on behalf of the hungry, I only have to remember Jesus pointing out the widow who gave her last pennies.

If we do this, God offers us as a contract: that he will always guide us, will satisfy our needs. But he offers more than this, much more... In the darkest times our country has seen for many years, God promises our light will rise. In the midst of fear and depression and anxiety, wondering if lockdowns will ever end, if we will be able to provide for our family, if we will catch or recover from this virus, we are promised that God will turn the bleakest night to noonday.

And finally:
If you keep your feet
from breaking the Sabbath
and from doing as you please
on my holy day,
if you call the Sabbath a delight
and the Lord's holy day honourable,
and if you honour it by not going your
own way and not doing as you please
or speaking idle words, then you will
find your joy in the Lord,
and I will cause you to ride in triumph on
the heights of the land and to feast on the
inheritance of your father Jacob.
Isaiah 58 v 13 to 14

This last contractual promise sums up God's blessing in my view. For some reason people struggle to take a day off, to rest, to trust that God will provide for us. Breaking the Sabbath does not mean that we've broken some archaic law, it means we've chosen to not accept that God will provide for us, chosen to believe we must work instead of trusting God to provide. And so the concept of fasting is flipped on its head. While I believe there is value in denying ourselves food for a time when choosing to humble ourselves before God, God's desire is that we choose each week to let him provide for us.

Our father in heaven, praise you that you want to provide for us, that you care so much for your people that you will not let us mistreat those around us. May we take the words of Isaiah to heart and seek to bring justice, to provide for those in need and seek to understand your Sabbath and allow ourselves to trust you completely. Amen.

Then he said "Jesus, remember me when you come into your kingdom." Jesus answered him, "Truly I tell you, today you will be with me in Paradise." Luke 23 v 42 to 43

Some hold the view that there are people who are too evil to be forgiven. Others believe they themselves have done things that can never be forgiven. Both are wrong.

King Ahab, along with his wife Jezebel, were considered two of the most evil rulers of Israel. 1 Kings 21 v 5 to 16 recounts an awful story of how Jezebel used a proclamation of a fast to entrap a man, have him killed and his vineyard stolen. God will hold anyone who behaves in such a manner accountable, especially someone in authority.

Yet even for someone as evil as King Ahab who conspired with Jezebel, God sees repentance and does not ignore it. No matter how evil you have been, there is always hope for you.

After being told God had judged Ahab and that he would be punished, we read:

When Ahab heard these words, he tore his clothes, put on sackcloth and fasted. He lay in sackcloth and went around meekly.

Then the word of the Lord came to Elijah the Tishbite: "Have you noticed how Ahab has humbled himself before me? Because he has humbled himself, I will not bring this disaster in his day, but I will bring it on his house in the days of his son."
1 Kings 21 v 27 to 29

God was not proposing to punish the son for the sins of the father, instead God knew that the son would choose to rebel against God and would reap his own punishment.

The interaction between Jesus and the prisoner hanging beside him on a cross shows God's great mercy to all of us. There was nothing that prisoner could do to deserve Jesus forgiveness. He had no ability to act in a different way, to show kindness to others, to demonstrate that his heart had changed, yet Jesus heard his plea for mercy and pardoned him and assured him he would join Jesus in paradise.

No matter what sin you have committed in the past, repent today and ask God's forgiveness. God is looking for each of us to humble ourselves, to acknowledge our weakness, to seek his forgiveness.

Our father in heaven, thank you for your great mercy. You do not treat us as we deserve, but to each one of us offer forgiveness through Jesus. May we humble ourselves, examine our hearts and actions, repent and seek your forgiveness. Thank you that you are quick to forgive! Amen.

…But each one should build with care. For no one can lay any foundation other than the one already laid, which is Jesus Christ. If anyone builds on this foundation using gold, silver, costly stones, wood, hay or straw, their work will be shown for what it is, because the Day will bring it to light.
It will be revealed with fire, and the fire will test the quality of each person's work. If what has been built survives, the builder will receive a reward. If it is burned up, the builder will suffer loss but yet will be saved— even though only as one escaping through the flames.
1 Corinthians 3 v 10 to 15

How do we know whether what we are building our lives with will survive? In Matthew 6, Jesus warned us to hide our "acts of righteousness": giving to the needy, praying, and fasting. What is done for God in secret will be rewarded on the day of judgement.

Though with each of these acts of righteousness, it is not just God who should be blessed, but also the world around us. We give so that those who are in need will share in our plenty, and sometimes so that they will share even with the little we have. We pray for God to transform the world around us, to guide our leaders, to bless our friends and family, but also our enemies! We are to forgive those who sin against us, as otherwise our own sins will not be forgiven. Our hearts are softened and humbled by this choice. So too when we fast, our whole body is humbled and our awareness of God and others around us is heightened.

Writing to the church in Corinth, in the passage above, Paul returns to a theme he often uses: Jesus Christ needs to be our true foundation. Jesus himself contrasted the wise and the foolish builder, the one who builds on bedrock, the one who builds on sand. Whether the coming judgement is fire or water, we are warned there will be consequences for the choices we make in life.

Will we choose to dig down through our lives, to expose our heart and thoughts, to allow Jesus to become the bedrock of our lives and build a new life on his foundation?

Are we building with gold, with silver, with costly stones? If so, and if I may mix the metaphors, we are told we will see fruit in this life as a result:

*"love, joy, peace, forbearance,
kindness, goodness, faithfulness,
gentleness and self-control."
Galatians 5 v 22 to 23*

Or are we building with the basest of materials that are destined to be consumed by fire? If so, there will be a different sort of fruit visible in our lives:

*"sexual immorality, impurity and
debauchery; idolatry and witchcraft;
hatred, discord, jealousy, fits of rage,
selfish ambition, dissensions, factions and
envy; drunkenness, orgies, and the like."
Galatians 5 v 19 to 21*

As he wrote these words to the Galatian church, Paul warned:

*"those who live like this will not inherit
the kingdom of God."
Galatians 5 v 21*

It is not enough to have Jesus as the foundation of our lives, we need to consider what we do each day, for each day adds to the previous day. Ever so slowly we are building something out of our lives. May we choose to build what will stand through into eternity.

Our father in heaven, make us aware of what we are "building" in and through our lives. Show us what will survive your fire of judgement, and what will be burnt up. Help us to choose to build what will be shown to be gold and silver and precious stones. Help us to seek the fruit of your spirit in our lives. Amen

Day 16   Blessings and Curses

However, if you do not obey
the Lord your God
and do not carefully follow all his
commands and decrees I am giving
you today, all these curses
will come on you and overtake you...
Deuteronomy 28 v 15

Hearing the news a number of years back, I was struck by a sense that the UK was experiencing curses such as those Israel were warned about before they entered the promised land of Canaan. God had led Israel out of slavery in Egypt and was about to fulfill a promise made centuries before to Abraham, that his descendants would live in Canaan and prosper there. But as with all important contracts, the promise was conditional. If Israel would be faithful in following God, would be obedient to his law, then they would receive many blessings. If not, then Israel risked having God remove his blessing and protection from them, and worse: the nation would be cursed.

A list of promised blessings and warnings of curses can be found in Deuteronomy 28. I felt sure there was a warning there about Israel becoming overrun with wild animals, that I was seeing a parallel between that and the reports of lone wolf terrorists that were attacking our cities. Yet when I went back and re-read the chapter there was no mention of wild animals.

Instead that warning is found in Leviticus 26, another place where God lays out his promise of blessings and warnings of curses:

'If you remain hostile toward me and refuse to listen to me, I will multiply your afflictions seven times over, as your sins deserve. I will send wild animals against you, and they will rob you of your children, destroy your cattle and make you so few in number that your roads will be deserted.'
Leviticus 26 v 21 to 22

As I read these chapters again, I am convicted. How is it that I and we ignore the promises of God?

'I will look on you with favour and make you fruitful and increase your numbers, and I will keep my covenant with you. You will still be eating last year's harvest when you will have to move it out to make room for the new. I will put my dwelling place among you, and I will not abhor you.'
Leviticus 26 v 9 to 11

God promises to protect and bless our families, our children. To prosper us so that the land will produce far more than we need. But far more than this, that God himself will live with us... We read the beginning of Genesis and see that God intended this world to be a paradise where he spent time with us. Some people would give all they possess to be able to meet and spend time with a celebrity, a sports star, a musician or performer. But the God who created these very people, who gave them their skills and gifts, who has done infinitely more, whose greatest performance brought this universe into being, this God offers to spend time with us.

Will we accept his offer? Will we seek his blessings and take heed of his warnings of what will happen to us if we do not?

Our father in heaven, may we seek and receive your blessings. May we read them, and also read of the curses that you warned would destroy Israel. May we turn from any disobedience and choose to follow you and your son Jesus. Thank you that in your mercy, you warn us of consequences and desire that we would choose you. Amen.

Day 17   Pray for our leaders

...as the king was walking on the roof of the royal palace of Babylon, he said, "Is not this the great Babylon I have built as the royal residence, by my mighty power and for the glory of my majesty?"
Even as the words were on his lips, a voice came from heaven,
"This is what is decreed for you, King Nebuchadnezzar: Your royal authority has been taken from you. You will be driven away from people and will live with the wild animals; you will eat grass like the ox. Seven times will pass by for you until you acknowledge that the Most High is sovereign over all kingdoms on earth and gives them to anyone he wishes."
Daniel 4 v 29 to 32

Over this last decade, it has often seemed to me that our leaders, at least in the UK, have been given over to a kind of madness. Strange decisions have been made, policies pursued that made no sense, holding referendums that risked breaking up the country, and ultimately did result in the UK leaving the EU.

I fear that God has given us the very leaders, and political opposition, that we deserve. That his judgement on us as a nation, his punishment, is to allow us to be led by people who reflect our hearts. You may support or despise our current leadership, either at a country or national level. You may have felt the same or differently about their predecessors. I wonder if our leaders have enacted what we collectively have wanted—a turning away from God, a descent into madness.

I live in Scotland and feel the independence movement at times displays the worst of Scotland. A deep resentment, that believes all of us in Scotland are victims of an English repression. That we have had our prosperity stolen from us, and we will never be wealthy until we've reclaimed our independence.

Prosperity though, comes to nations that follow God's law. Scotland, and indeed the UK, used to value the reading of the bible. Our entire education system grew out of a desire and need to study God's word. And as ordinary men and women studied and applied God's commands to their lives, the nations of the UK grew wealthy.

I confess that I have not often prayed for our leaders. Yet this is an instruction I must make an effort to follow. Jesus told us to show love to our enemies. If we despise those who rule over us, this reveals our sinful hearts. As Paul writes:

I urge, then, first of all, that petitions, prayers, intercession and thanksgiving be made for all people--for kings and all those in authority, that we may live peaceful and quiet lives in all godliness and holiness. This is good, and pleases God our Saviour, who wants all people to be saved and to come to a knowledge of the truth.
1 Timothy 2 v 1 to 4

I've seen too many images of riots in previously orderly cities this last year. I have a temper myself, I know what it feels like to let go to rage. Yet I would far rather restrain that part of me than live with the consequences of destruction. Our world is going through a time of upheaval. Would you rather live in a godless and wicked society, or one where the people around you respect and fear God, and are conscious of and respectful of consequences? Do you want to live a peaceful life? If so, pray for our leaders.

Our father in heaven, you appoint leaders to rule over us. We ask that you will not give us the leaders we deserve, but instead give us leaders who will lead us towards you. May our leaders be convicted of their need for you, soften their hearts that they will call out to you for wisdom and will accept your guidance. Deliver our leaders from sin, lead them from evil and into your truth. Amen.

Day 18   Repent and turn to God

"Repent, then, and turn to God, so that your sins may be wiped out, that times of refreshing may come from the Lord, and that he may send the Messiah, who has been appointed for you--even Jesus."
Acts 3 v 19 to 20

Debt can be crippling. Like a great weight pressing down on us, crushing us and preventing us from breathing. The knowledge that you owe something that cannot be repaid can destroy a person. It is no surprise that sin is often characterised as a debt.

Yet God has no desire to hold our debts against us. Again and again we are told to repent, to turn to God, and always the promise is there: "so that your sins may be wiped out"!

I've been fortunate enough to rarely have needed to take out a loan, but just over a decade ago, we felt we needed to in order to afford a car. At the time the monthly payments seemed affordable, but we were stuck with the debt for five years and every month that payment had to be made otherwise we risked losing the car and worse, additional interest payments being added on top. When we finally paid the last payment, I swore never again! I've heard stories of people who have received a gift, allowing them to repay their debts, to be set free. I can imagine the relief and release that comes with such a blessing. Indeed, I've experienced it myself in finding forgiveness from my own sin…

To know you are guilty, to know you deserve no forgiveness, but then to have forgiveness offered freely, to realise that all that is asked of you is to turn back to God, to turn away from your previous sin… To accept and receive that wiping out of the debt of sin is to be relieved of a great weight, is to find you can stand freely, your lungs able to fill fully again. As Charles Wesley wrote in his great hymn: And can it be that I should gain:

My chains fell off, my heart was free,
I rose, went forth, and followed Thee.

Look back at the words of Peter. He calls all to repent and turn to God. He promises your sin will be wiped out, that times of refreshing will be given from the Lord. But more than that, far more, he suggests that our repentance will finally cause God to send Jesus back to us. May each of us examine our heart, repent and turn to God, and receive the blessing and promise God offers us.

Our father in heaven, thank you does not seem enough to say. You save us from a crippling debt we cannot pay, you set us free through Jesus, you refresh us, and more: you promise Jesus will return for us. Praise you! Bless you! May we respond with gratefulness to your kindness. Amen.

Day 19   Mercy and compassion

"I will have mercy on whom I have mercy,
and I will have compassion on
whom I have compassion."
Romans 9 v 15

In writing to the Romans, Paul reveals his great sorrow that many of his countrymen are destined for destruction. Even though God promised to make Israel his own people, their rebellion had cut them off from God. Then, to make matters infinitely worse, Israel rejected God's son, his only son who was sent to save them. The killing of Jesus by Israel was to lead in a few short decades to Israel's destruction. However, God has mercy on whom he will have mercy!

Despite the killing of his son, God still caused Jesus disciples to call Israel back to repentance. Many in Israel at that time did repent, did turn back to God and accept Jesus. But God was not content with that, he sent Jesus disciples and new believers out from Israel to the gentile nations surrounding them.

The message of Jesus was not just to offer mercy to Israel, but to all people everywhere.

If you read through the book of Acts, you see a disturbing pattern. As Paul went to each new gentile city, some of the Jews living there would take offence and have Paul thrown out, or beaten, and they even attempted to kill him. Is it possible these people could not accept that God no longer wanted to treat only Israel as his own nation, but instead wanted to offer all people the same mercy? Is it possible that like a true born son threatened by the possibility the adopted child would split the inheritance, that they acted in this way? If so, these Jews failed to understand that God's inheritance will not be lessened, it is so vast that all people can benefit from it with no-one going without.

What should our response be to God's great mercy? Paul goes on to write:

Therefore, I urge you, brothers and sisters, in view of God's mercy, to offer your bodies as a living sacrifice, holy and pleasing to God— this is your true and proper worship. Do not conform to the pattern of this world, but be transformed by the renewing

of your mind. Then you will be able to test and approve what God's will is--his good, pleasing and perfect will.
Romans 12 v 1 to 2

As Jesus wrote, love the Lord your God with all your heart and soul and mind, we are to offer all of ourselves as a living sacrifice, each day given to God, even our very thoughts renewed and transformed.

Our father in heaven, may we not read or say these words glibly, but may we let them change us. As we have received your mercy and compassion, may we give our lives back to you in thankfulness. May we give each day to you, even allow you to transform our thoughts. Thank you for your promise that as we do this, you reveal your good, pleasing and perfect will to us! Amen.

~~~~~~~~~~~~~~~~~~~~~~~~~~~~~~

Day 20   The Redeemer will come

~~~~~~~~~~~~~~~~~~~~~~~~~~~~~~

"The Redeemer will come to Zion,
to those in Jacob who repent of their sins,"
declares the Lord.
Isaiah 59 v 20

Why doesn't God answer? Why will he not help me? The prophet Isaiah had this message for Israel:

Surely the arm of the Lord is not
too short to save, nor his ear
too dull to hear.
But your iniquities have
Separated you from your God;
your sins have hidden his face from
you, so that he will not hear.
For your hands are stained with blood,
your fingers with guilt.
Your lips have spoken falsely, and
your tongue mutters wicked things.
Isaiah 59 v 1 to 3

God is ready, willing and able to save us. He is not distant from us or unable to hear when we cry out to him. Yet it is within our power to push God away from us.

There are terms in God's word that I only have a vague understanding of. Iniquity is one such word. What does it really mean?

The Chambers dictionary includes the following definitions:

- A lack of fairness and justice
- Gross injustice
- Wickedness
- Sin
- A crime
- Scandalously unreasonable...

When we behave like this, we push God away from us, and God will allow us to.

When we sin, God will turn from us and will stop listening to us.

Are our hands stained with blood, are our hands stained with guilt? I read this and cannot help but think of the 200,000 unborn babies who are killed each year in the UK. Are any of us free of that guilt?

Have our lips spoken falsely, have we muttered wicked things? It seems to me to be quite a contrast between murder and muttering, yet both, and everything in between creates a gulf between us and God. We are separated from God and it is entirely our fault.

However, always there is hope…

Isaiah went on to write that the redeemer, the one who pays the price to set you free, will come to those who repent of their sins. Repent. Turn from your sin. Turn to God and he will hear you, he will stretch out his hand to save you.

Our father in heaven, thank you that you are not far from us, that you are waiting for each one of us to turn from sin and turn back to you. May we heed your call, may we respond quickly. Deliver us from sin in our life and set us free. Amen.

But the wicked are like the tossing sea, which cannot rest, whose waves cast up mire and mud. "There is no peace," says my God, "for the wicked."
Isaiah 57 v 20 to 21

"There is no peace," says my God, "for the wicked." These words, recorded by the prophet Isaiah, come at the end of a passage where God promises he will not always punish those who show repentance. Read them again, meditate on them. There is no peace for the wicked.

But you probably already know this. I certainly do. If I believe I am guilty, I cannot rest, I cannot relax. I'm haunted until I confess. Until I make an effort to put right what was wrong.

Fortunately, most times, we can make amends, can apologise. There is always a cost, whether a knock to our pride, or sometimes much more serious. Some mistakes cannot be fixed. Some have consequences that will stay with us the rest of our lives. Yet I would rather accept those consequences in trying to apologise and repair what has been done than live without peace.

I get the sense though that wickedness is a choice not to repent. A choice to, in one respect, bury sin and refuse to face the consequences. In another, to continue in sin. In this sense, wickedness is rebellion against God.

Isaiah ends the prophetic book with a final warning against those who rebel:

"From one New Moon to another
and from one Sabbath to another, all
mankind will come and bow down before
me," says the Lord.
"And they will go out and look on the
dead bodies of those who rebelled against
me; the worms that eat them will not die,
the fire that burns them will
not be quenched, and they will be
loathsome to all mankind."
Isaiah 66 v 23 to 24

This is an image that Jesus repeated several times, and later we see the reference to worms and fire tormenting for ever added to the end of the prophecy of Revelation. Those who opposed God and those whose names were not written in the book of life are to be thrown into the lake of eternal fire.

We always have a choice. Rebel against God, or repent and turn back to him. And for those who do repent and turn back:

Praise be to the God and Father of our Lord Jesus Christ, the Father of compassion and the God of all comfort, who comforts us in all our troubles, so that we can comfort those in any trouble with the comfort we ourselves receive from God.
2 Corinthians 1 v 3 to 4

If you are not at peace, if you know you cannot rest for sin in your life, then turn to Jesus, confess your sin, and ask for his help to deal with that sin.

Our father in heaven, may we seek your peace. Deliver us from fear and pride and enable us to turn from any wickedness in our life. Give us the courage to confess sin and make amends to any we have hurt. Give us your peace and your rest. Amen.

.

"You have heard that it was said, 'Love your neighbour and hate your enemy.' But I tell you, love your enemies and pray for those who persecute you, that you may be children of your Father in heaven. He causes his sun to rise on the evil and the good, and sends rain on the righteous and the unrighteous. If you love those who love you, what reward will you get?"
Matthew 5 v 43 to 46

Do you have any enemies? I imagine for many this might seem rather theoretical. We live fairly peaceful lives, get on with those we work with, greet our neighbours, perhaps we're even fortunate enough to like our wider family...

Even if this does describe you, I suspect you are not far off having had or having enemies in your life.

School can be a harsh place for many children. If we could listen in on all their conversations, we'd find many children who are cruel, even those who think they need to be in order to defend a friend.

Family feuds can fester for generations. Lack of contact can hide animosity, and sometimes we can choose to disguise our hatred when face to face.

A busy office or any type of workplace can have multiple conflicts taking place at many levels. I've been shocked to find company messaging applications used to carry on arguments and accusations, spreading rumours out of sight of one's line managers.

Then, even in the most idyllic settings, neighbours can take offence, can oppose your plans, or work to undermine your reputation.

Sometimes we create our enemies, sometimes they choose that role for themselves.

I've been challenged by Jesus words many times. Neighbours who used to play loud music until the early hours of the morning, no matter how many times I went round and asked them to stop. I eventually had to learn to lie in bed, praying for God to bless them. After a couple of years, we found it possible to move house. I was able to leave without bitterness.

I remember colleagues who passively ignored my requests for help or information, or actively were aggressive. I heard someone teach once that you should ask God to bless difficult colleagues with a promotion or new job. I started doing this, but also just praying for them. I found my attitude changed. I also started noticing some of those people moving to new roles and jobs...

It is not easy to choose to pray blessing on someone or a group who is causing your problems or pain. But Jesus never said following him would be easy, instead he was at pains to warn his disciples how difficult it would be. Each of us at one time was, or still is, an enemy of Jesus. Jesus chose to love us, chose to leave heaven and bless us, chose to accept all and any punishment that we deserved when he died on the cross. This is how the Prince of Peace treated his enemies. Will you ask him to help you do the same?

Our father in heaven, I can only thank you that when I was still your enemy, Jesus came to make peace with me. Help me to show the same love that Jesus showed me, to my enemies. May I choose to bless them, to seek your goodness for them, to let my heart be changed to love them. Amen.

Day 23 Those who sleep in the dust

Multitudes who sleep in the dust of the earth will awake: some to everlasting life, others to shame and everlasting contempt. Those who are wise will shine like the brightness of the heavens, and those who lead many to righteousness, like the stars for ever and ever.
Daniel 12 v 2 to 3

Some people argue that this life is all there is. They would contend there are no consequences for what we do, no final judgement. They mock saying there is no "pie in the sky", no need to fear demons with pitchforks. Paul was very aware of this belief, writing to the Corinthian church:

If only for this life we have hope in Christ, we are of all people most to be pitied.
1 Corinthians 15 v 19

If you read through the whole of the Old Testament, you could be forgiven for wondering where the idea of life after death came from. It just doesn't show up, not until the book of Daniel anyway. But then it's tossed in like a grenade. I love the language he uses. Multitudes... who are sleeping in the dust... then we all wake and some of us are jumping out of that grave, others may never want to leave it...

Rewards or punishment await us all. I've always admired wisdom and would love to have been judged as having been wise like Solomon was at his best. To have led many others to righteousness, to have these people surround you with gladness, all of you knowing that your reward is eternal, the full life Jesus described, this is what you have to look forward to, if in this life you are wise...

Jesus even challenged the concept of death when he said of his father:

"He is not the God of the dead,
but of the living."
Mark 12 v 27

It is not for no reason the early church described those who had died as having fallen asleep! What we do in this life has eternal consequences. I do not want to even imagine waking up to shame and everlasting contempt. It is worth fighting for righteousness now, it is worth suffering now, is worth persevering now, disciplining yourself now, because this life is not all that there is.

Our father in heaven, give us an eternal perspective. Help us to understand that our actions and words do not just affect this life, but our future in the life to come. May we choose wisely, and seek your eternal reward. Amen.

Day 24   The power of the kingdom

*"...I tell you, among those born of women
there is no one greater than John;
yet the one who is least in the kingdom
of God is greater than he."*
Luke 7 v 28

It is a dreadful thing to be depressed, to feel you have no hope, to doubt your life has been worthwhile. Imagine if you have sacrificed everything, dedicated your life to a cause, and then are unsure whether you made any difference at all. Such seems to have been the experience of John the Baptist. There are two accounts that suggest his state of mind in Luke 7 and Matthew 11. Only Matthew reveals that John was in prison. No comfortable cell for him. No mandatory exercise in the fresh air, no skills training. He would have starved if not for his followers who brought him food. He may have been chained all day and night, forced to relieve himself where he slept. He may not have seen daylight for weeks or even months. All this after spending his life in the desert, forgoing luxury and comfort and inviting mockery and insult, all so he could warn people to get ready, that the one who would save Israel was about to be revealed. It seems John doubted whether Jesus was indeed the one he had been waiting for. Look at the message John had preached:

> *"Repent, for the kingdom of heaven*
> *has come near."*
> *Matthew 3 v 1*

John was waiting for the kingdom of heaven to be revealed, expecting something amazing, but we don't know exactly what John expected. It's possible John himself did not know. God does not always tell his prophets why they should give a certain message, after all why should the king have to share all his plans with his servants?

John was looking for signs of the kingdom of heaven, desperate to know his life, his suffering had not been in vain. And how did Jesus respond?

> *...he replied to the messengers,*
> *"Go back and report to John what you*

*have seen and heard: The blind receive
sight, the lame walk, those who have
leprosy are cleansed, the deaf hear,
the dead are raised, and the good news
is proclaimed to the poor..."*
Luke 7 v 22

These are all signs of the kingdom of
heaven. Miracles that transform peoples' lives,
and the preaching of good news to the poor.
And then Jesus gave one final message to
John:

*"Blessed is the man who does not
stumble on account of me."*
Luke 7 v 23

Jesus did not break John out of prison. He
may not have delivered John from his state of
depression, if that was what John was
experiencing. No, he sent a message to John
to hold firm, to believe the evidence John's
disciples would have seen and heard. Jesus
trusted that John could choose to keep
believing, and that that would be enough.

If you feel this cruel, remember, Jesus knew
his own destiny. John would not experience
any worse than Jesus knew he would face. As

Jesus said many times, a servant is no greater than his master. And if we choose to follow Jesus, we also are his servants...

John was a great man. He rightly has been remembered and as Jesus said: "...among those born of women there is no one greater than John..." Yet Jesus seems to imply that John was not living in the kingdom of God, possibly because John was the last prophet before Jesus: "...yet the one who is least in the kingdom of God is greater than he."

This is the position we are in. Jesus the saviour has been revealed, and he did not just come to save Israel, but to save people around the world. The kingdom of heaven is here and will be our kingdom—if we will submit ourselves to its king: Jesus.

Our father in heaven, may we not lose heart. No matter what trouble overwhelms us, may we turn to Jesus and believe the testimony of his disciples in your word. May we hold onto the promises of Jesus, may we submit to Jesus, to you, and acknowledge you as our king. Amen.

Day 25   It's impossible!

"…unless you repent,
you too will all perish."
Luke 13 v 3

Many are familiar with Jesus warning that it is easier for a camel to go through the eye of a needle than for the rich to enter the kingdom of God. The disciples heard this, were astonished and then asked: "Who then can be saved?" Jesus answer gives hope:

Jesus looked at them and said,
"With man this is impossible, but with
God all things are possible."
Matthew 19 v 25 to 26

Jesus came to do the impossible. Things that even today people are sceptical of: restoring sight to the blind, returning hearing to the deaf, enabling the cripple and the lame to walk, and of course, bringing the dead back to life. No wonder drugs used, no medical interventions or CPR, just a half dozen impossible things before breakfast, and possibly a few dozen more before lunch.

Yet there were times when Jesus could not do quite as many impossible healings, places where people lacked faith. It was not for a lack of willingness on Jesus part. Jesus wanted to heal. Just as he wants to gather as many of us as he can into his kingdom. If we will let him... If we will make the effort.

Jesus warned again and again it is not easy to follow him. Luke records him warning:

"Make every effort to enter through the narrow door, because many, I tell you, will try to enter and will not be able to. Once the owner of the house gets up and closes the door, you will stand outside knocking and pleading, 'Sir, open the door for us.'
"But he will answer, 'I don't know you or where you come from.'"
Luke 13 v 24 to 25

Our entry into the kingdom of God is not a given. Some of us are sleepwalking our way to death. Jesus was told about a tragedy, cruel murders and desecration of the bodies. The thinking seems to have been that those people were worse sinners, more evil than others to have died in such a way. Jesus kills this concept dead and then goes on to say: "But unless you repent, you too will all perish." No matter how perfect our lives appear on the outside, or how evil, we are all in need of Jesus' mercy. But when we realise how much we need God's mercy, this can be overwhelming! Paul sums it up well:

What a wretched man I am!
Who will rescue me from this body
that is subject to death?
Romans 7 v 24

Paul then goes on to share one of the most wonderful messages any of us can hear! Firstly that we can thank God that our rescuer is Jesus Christ our Lord! Then we read these beautiful words:

Therefore, there is now no condemnation
for those who are in Christ Jesus, because
through Christ Jesus the law of the Spirit
who gives life has set you free
from the law of sin and death.
Romans 8 v 1 to 2

And Paul continues, to share a message of

great hope:

And we know that in all things God works
for the good of those who love him, who
have been called according to his purpose.
v 28

If God is for us, who can be against us.
v 31

He who did not spare his own Son,
but gave him up for us all—
how will he not also, along with him,
graciously give us all things?
v 32

Who will bring any charge against those
whom God has chosen? It is God who
justifies. Who then is the one who
condemns? No one. Christ Jesus who
died--more than that, who was raised to
life--is at the right hand of God and is also
interceding for us. Who shall separate us
from the love of Christ? Shall trouble or
hardship or persecution or famine
or nakedness or danger or sword?
v 33 to 35

No, in all these things we are more than conquerors through him who loved us. For I am convinced that neither death nor life, neither angels nor demons, neither the present nor the future, nor any powers, neither height nor depth, nor anything else in all creation, will be able to separate us from the love of God that is in Christ Jesus our Lord.
v 37 to 39

Are you in Christ Jesus? Do you have the assurance that Paul describes here? If not, do you want it?

Our father in heaven, thank you for your great gift through Jesus Christ. I will follow you, I will follow your son, Jesus. I recognise that I can do nothing to earn my salvation, but I ask you to forgive me, to cleanse me of my sin, to accept me into your kingdom. Where my faith is weak, strengthen my faith. Guide me and lead me and help me to believe the promises of Jesus are for me. Amen.

Day 26 Whatever you do

Slaves, obey your earthly masters in everything; and do it, not only when their eye is on you and to curry their favour, but with sincerity of heart and reverence for the Lord. Whatever you do, work at it with all your heart, as working for the Lord, not for human masters, since you know that you will receive an inheritance from the Lord as a reward. It is the Lord Christ you are serving.
Colossians 3 v 22 to 24

Who would want to be a slave? Despite laws abolishing slavery, some estimate there are still tens of millions of slaves worldwide and thousands more than we might expect here in the UK. Having been brought up in a supposedly free society, the fact that God's word has laws for treatment of slaves can be hard to reconcile. Does God condone slavery?

It was never God's intention for his people to be slaves, indeed God sent Moses to free the slaves from Egypt. Yet slavery was not condemned outright. It may not have been acceptable for the children of Israel to be slaves, but it was acceptable for them to own slaves.

Most of my life, I've read the term slave and interpreted it as employee. I've never been a slave and at least for most in the UK, slavery was outlawed long ago. But there are useful lessons to learn from the laws on ownership and treatment of slaves from God's word, and from instruction to slaves like the passage above.

It's easy to work hard when our work is enjoyable. Our jobs may sometimes be boring and monotonous, may require backbreaking work, may seem pointless. It is tempting, if we are given a chance, to slack off. You may not have a slave master watching over you, but you may work for someone who does watch what you do, who perhaps measures how much you produce, how fast you work, what the quality of your work is...

Do we obey our employers in everything?

Do we obey them even when we are not being watched?

Do we have the attitude that whatever our work, we will give our all, as if we were working for the Lord?

Do we understand there is a reward for those who do work as if working for the Lord, that those who would otherwise have received no inheritance, will receive an inheritance from the Lord?

Jesus preached a kingdom that seemed upside down to the kingdoms of this world. Repentance can sometimes mean continuing to do everything you did before, but with a changed heart. Allowing yourself to feel joy despite drudgery, to show patience despite irritation, being kind to those who do not deserve it, forgiving those who hurt and wound.

Mahatma Gandhi is said to have stated: "You can chain me, you can torture me, you can even destroy this body, but you will never imprison my mind." Powerful words proclaiming that even slavery does not have to mean we are defeated. Yet almost two thousand years previously, Jesus followers taught a much more daring message. Regardless of your circumstances, serve as if you are serving God. Work hard even when you are not being watched. Obey with a sincere heart.

Our father in heaven, praise you for the opportunity to work and serve. Bless the work of my hands. Bless my employer and my colleagues. Deliver me from laziness, from resentment, from ungratefulness. May I see your glory, even in the mess of my life and work. Help me to serve you in all I do. Amen.

Day 27   Open your ears and eyes

*"'Go to this people and say,
"You will be ever hearing but never understanding; you will be ever seeing but never perceiving."
For this people's heart has become calloused; they hardly hear with their ears, and they have closed their eyes.
Otherwise they might see with their eyes, hear with their ears, understand with their hearts and turn, and I would heal them.'
Acts 28 v 26 to 27*

It is easy to harden our hearts, to close our eyes and turn away from those we don't want to listen to. Much harder to keep listening, to look intently, and humble our attitude to consider what is being said.

I've never found it easy to admit I'm wrong. There have been many times when I've been wrong and my refusal to admit it has not changed anything, just delayed the point at which I've had to face the consequences. Over

the years I've found it better to admit to my
failures and mistakes sooner, though I still
find it a struggle.

Paul said the words above to the Jewish
leaders in Rome. The writer records that some
of the Jewish leaders believed Paul's message
that Jesus was the son of God promised
through the prophets, others did not. I get a
sense of deep frustration in Paul's words. But
it is difficult to know exactly why Paul said
them. During the Coronavirus pandemic, I
think we've all become more aware of how
much of a role facial expression plays in
conveying meaning. Wearing a mask prevents
us from communicating effectively. Even the
tone of our voice can change the meaning of
words.

I believe Paul cared deeply for his Jewish
brothers. He had almost been killed several
times in his efforts to share the good news of
Jesus with them in other cities. It is recorded:

*"He witnessed to them from morning till
evening..."*
Acts 28 v 23

Paul was willing to give all his time, his
energy, even—if necessary—his life for the

Jews. He knew the Jews were about to face dreadful consequences. They had rejected Jesus, the very son of God. The consequence was to be the destruction of Jerusalem and the scattering of the Jewish nation for almost two thousand years.

Yet even in these words of frustration there is a message of hope. If, even at this last minute, they were to turn back to God, he would heal them. This is a message of hope that we need to take heed of. In scattering the Jewish nation, God turned to us, the Gentiles, and offered us the same good news Jesus had offered to the Jews. We in this country have the same choice they were given: turn to God, listen to his son Jesus, seek his kingdom and the righteousness that comes through faith in Jesus. We can choose to soften our hearts. Will you?

Our father in heaven, have mercy on us, have mercy on our nation! Open our eyes, soften our hearts that we might see you, and see our sin. Open our ears that we will understand what you have to say to us, and that we will turn back to you, and be healed by you! Amen.

Day 28   Live by the Spirit

So I say, live by the Spirit, and you will not gratify the desires of the flesh.
Galatians 5 v 16

I had an experience of being filled by the Holy Spirit when I was twenty. It seemed at that time to turn my life around. Looking back, it now seems similar to falling in love. I had fallen in love with God. But as most people who fall in love find out, that initial buzz and feeling can fade. It is not that you have fallen out of love, though if the feeling is all you have based love on, it may seem like that. Instead, I think that for me, I had taken that love for granted. God was still in love with me, I just hadn't made the effort to habitually, consistently, deliberately love him back.

I have a "study" bible, one that has commentary on some verses and passages. A gift from my wife from before we were married, and still one of my most treasured possessions. The commentary on the verse above suggests that the word "live" can also be translated "go on living". Living by the spirit is intentional. It is a daily choice. Sometimes a choice we have to make hour by hour or minute by minute. Just like marriage... Any marriage where one or both partners fail to choose to show love to each other on an ongoing basis is one that is precarious.

What does it mean to go on living by the spirit? Paul goes on to refer to being "led by the spirit". In a good marriage, each partner will lead each other onto better things. Encouraging each other, supporting each other, guiding each other.

I was going to write that the Holy Spirit does not need our encouragement... But then I don't know if that is true. God desires a relationship with us. I don't believe for a minute that God simply wants to tell us everything and all that we should do. My understanding is that God does want to guide us, but also is eager to see and be part of what we choose to do. I've certainly noticed as my own children have grown that I'm delighted when they make choices off their own back that I can see are good ones.

Paul encourages us to:

"…keep in step with the spirit"
v 25

Partners in a marriage do not have to always agree, but it is important to keep in step with each other. This may mean ensuring that our partner is enabled to live as fulfilling a life as we are able to. It may mean rejecting some opportunities as the life long relationship is more important than a short term gain. It certainly means discussing what has happened, what is happening, and what we want to happen in the future! God is completely open about what he wants out of our relationship, and what he offers to us. Both Abraham and Moses negotiated with God and within reason, we can do the same.

What are the desires of the flesh? In my now outdated copy of the bible this is translated: sinful nature. Well, Paul goes on to list a number of "acts" of the flesh. Desire often leads to action. Why is it important that we don't turn these desires into action? Paul spells it out:

I warn you, as I did before, that those who
live like this will not inherit
the kingdom of God.
Galatians 5 v 21

Sometimes we need things spelt out as bluntly as possibly. Just as there are severe consequences for someone in a marriage who betrays their vows, there are severe consequences for us if we reject God's Holy Spirit.

Our father in heaven, may we fall in love with you. May we understand and realise how much you love us. May we receive the presence of your Spirit in us, and may we be intentional in maintaining our relationship with you, through your Holy Spirit. Amen.

Day 29   Love one another

My command is this:
Love each other as I have loved you.
Greater love has no one than this:
to lay down one's life for one's friends.
You are my friends if you do
what I command.
John 15 v 12 to 14

I fear that our culture has little understanding of the concept that is love. As a child I was taught that the Greek language had three distinct words for love: eros, philia, and agape. Eros encompassing romantic through to sexual love which seems to be how most people interpret love today. Philia describing friendship, companionship and family relationships. Yet above and beyond both of these was agape: a sacrificial love, selfless, serving, unconditional. The deepest and most daring of all three. Indeed, without agape, can either eros, or philia be considered true love?

If we read Jesus words in the Greek, we

find here he was talking about agape love.
Immediately before he taught his disciples, we
see that he chose to demonstrate this form of
love in a striking way, shedding his role as
respected teacher, as their leader, and
becoming the lowest of all servants, washing
the feet of his disciples. This selfless act
became a bookend along with his freely given
sacrifice of his life, allowing himself to be
arrested, to be tortured, and killed in our
place. Jesus showed his agape love for his
disciples in a simple and yet powerful gesture,
then for the whole world in the ultimate
sacrificial act.

And in between these two acts of agape
love, Jesus shared the most powerful teaching
on love. Jesus wanted each of us to learn and
understand something fundamental about
how we should live our lives. You will be
aware there were ten commandments given by
God to Moses. Jesus was now giving a single
new command to everyone who would follow
him, who would become part of his new
kingdom: Love one another. Love each other
as Jesus loved you. How did he love us? He
laid down his life, becoming a servant, and
ultimately sacrificing himself.

To become a disciple of Jesus is to be

obedient to him, but we are not just called to be followers, we are called to be his friends. Yet just as being a disciple is conditional on our obedience to Jesus, his offer of friendship is conditional on us choosing to lay down our lives for those around us.

We may not be called on to lose our lives to save others, though some will, and may God give courage and love to those who have to make that ultimate sacrifice. For the rest of us, how we will need to lay down our lives will differ depending on who is in our lives, and what their needs are.

Our father in heaven, thank you for Jesus, for his demonstration of love towards us. Thank you that his command is good and benefits us and everyone around us. Jesus, thank you that you showed yourself to be our friend, laying down your life so that we could have eternal life. Help us to follow you, to show love for others as you showed to us. Amen.

Day 30   The right to the tree of life

Blessed are those who wash their robes,
that they may have the right to the tree of
life and may go through the gates
into the city.
Revelation 22 v 14

At the end of John's vision recorded in the book of Revelation, he sees heaven coming down to earth in the form of a beautiful city, shining like a precious jewel. But while the streets of this city will be made of pure gold, it is a city with life growing and flowing out of it. Out of the city will flow…

"…the river of the water of life…"
v 1

…and on opposite banks of this river stand the tree of life.

There was a tree of life at the beginning of time, and God would not let us eat the fruit because we rebelled against him and chose instead to seek the knowledge of good and evil. God is recorded as saying that if we ate this fruit we would live for ever.

I struggle with the concept of living for ever. It seems that many of us do. Yet I want it. The fruit of the tree of life was not forbidden in the beginning. It seems it was God's desire from the start that we should live and never die.

If only Adam and Eve had not given into temptation, what would this world look like today? John possibly had a vision of that. He tells of a new earth and a new heaven. And we can see what John saw, if we will only "wash our robes".

Jesus had this to say about a man who did not wash his robes before attending a wedding feast:

"Tie him hand and foot, and throw him outside, into the darkness, where there will be weeping and gnashing of teeth." 'For many are invited, but few are chosen.' Matthew 22 v 13 to 14

You are invited to the wedding feast in heaven, and just as I would hope you would prepare before attending a wedding here on earth, you would be wise to prepare for this final wedding. How do we wash our robes?

- Through confession of sin
- Through repentance
- Through believing in Jesus
- Through receiving the Holy Spirit

At times Jesus spoke plainly so children could understand. At other times he seemed to speak in riddles, deliberately so only his followers would understand, and sometimes only after he explained to them. When Jesus declared in John 3 v 3: "Very truly I tell you, no one can see the kingdom of God unless they are born again.", it confused his listener, and still confuses many today.

I believe Jesus was speaking of a change that takes place when any person decides to follow Jesus. In the game of poker, it is equivalent to going all in. There is no half-hearted follower of Jesus. It is all or nothing. Jesus asks for all we have. I write this knowing that I have not lived up to these words. But I believe Jesus knew I would fail, knew I would turn back, just as he knew Peter would deny him, that the other disciples would flee when he was arrested.

It is not for a single day that Jesus told us to

ask God to forgive us our sins. It is not for nothing that Jesus told his disciples they should forgive their brothers seventy times seven.

I do not believe repentance is a one time event. I believe it is continual, deliberate, intentional. It is the alcoholic who has reached thirty eight years, two months and seventeen days still making the same choice to avoid or turn down the offer of a drink. It is also that same alcoholic who gave in three days later, and starts again at the beginning, refusing to let one slip up rule his life from then on.

As a young man I experienced a filling of the Holy Spirit that transformed me. I indeed felt as if I had been born again. However, I have found myself having to repent many times since then. My robes are often in need of washing. I will continue to follow Jesus, continue to confess sin, to repent, continue to believe that Jesus loves me far more than I can comprehend, continue to seek the filling of his Holy Spirit. I pray that you, reading this, will do the same.

Our father in heaven, give us a vision of eternal life with you, of healing from sickness and infirmity, of a new earth for us to share with you. Help us to understand what it will mean for us to wash our robes and prepare for life with you. Give us the courage to choose to follow you, no matter what cost. Amen.

Day 31   What do you do next?

*Very early in the morning,
while it was still dark,
Jesus got up, left the house and went
off to a solitary place, where he prayed.*
Mark 1 v 35

Well done! You've reached the end of this challenge to spend 31 days in prayer. Perhaps you have started to wonder, what next?

I'd like you to take a few minutes asking God what you should do next and waiting for him to speak. Then turn the page and I'll have some closing comments for you…

What did God tell you? I'd love for you to share with me what he said. You can write to me at mark@dragonlake.co.uk

If though, you didn't hear God tell you anything, don't be discouraged! I frequently find myself failing to hear anything when I ask God to speak. I've come to believe this is not because I'm some sort of failure, or that God doesn't want to speak to me, but instead that for most of us, most of the time, God expects us to have the wit to make a decision as to what we should do with our time.

God didn't create us in his image so he'd have to hand hold us through every choice we make. I believe God desires a relationship with us, one where God is just as intrigued and fascinated to find out what we think as we are to find out what he thinks. I do believe God directs us and will give us advice and will speak to us, but my experience suggests that he trusts us to tell the difference between good and evil. After all, the reason we're separated from God in the first place is because we chose the knowledge of good and evil…

Of course, sometimes we choose evil over good, and in part, that's why I wrote this 31 day prayer challenge. Because while God trusts us to choose, there are consequences for choosing evil. Repentance is the choice to turn from evil back to God, and to seek him so that we can choose good instead.

Since we are to follow Jesus, we should look to his example. It was his custom to get up early and go to a solitary place and pray. This is a valuable habit to develop, one I'm still working on!

While we were dating, my wife Teri, shared that she was reading the bible from beginning to end. I was challenged by this, despite having been raised by Christian parents, attending church meetings sometimes three or four times a week, I'd never read the bible cover to cover. Teri was following a method where you start reading single chapters from the book of Genesis and Isaiah, one from each book each day, continuing until you've read every book of the bible. If you've never committed to reading the bible daily, it is a challenge, but considering how many in the West spend their time, it is perfectly achievable. I found by sticking with this routine, I gained a much greater appreciation of how the different books of the bible relate. That there is a clear story arc from Genesis through to Revelation of God's love for us, and many, many sub plots.

There are several versions of reading the bible in a year, some of which will take you through in order of events, others which focus on specific themes. As well as physical books you can buy, there are now multiple apps you can download onto your Smartphone or tablet which will prompt you each day to read specific verses or chapters.

I do believe that when I'm consistent at spending time in prayer to God, when I consistently read his word, my relationship with God improves, as does my attitude in general, and my relationships with others.

Some people believe a habit can be formed in as little as a month, or 31 days, though from what I've read, habit forming is different for each person and can take anywhere from a few weeks to many months. I would be delighted if you were to use this book as a springboard to continue to seek the kingdom of heaven, to live in repentance, and to continue in daily building your relationship with God.

Our father in heaven, thank you that you hear our prayers, that you also talk back, if we are willing to listen. Thank you for your word, for the encouragement and challenges we find there. May we continue to seek you, to live in repentance, and develop a closer relationship with you. Amen.

The story of this book

31 Days of Prayer was originally published as an eBook and in reviewing it for this print edition I felt the original introduction was too long and distracted from the intention. If you are curious as to why it came to be written I include that introduction below…

As I write I see there have been over two million deaths worldwide from a new corona virus. Over 100 million affected, that we know about. Leaders in many countries around the world have tried to stem the rise in infections with different tactics which have had debatable effect. Country wide lockdowns, panic and confusion, uncertainty over the future have all led to mass unemployment and soaring poverty.

When this new plague took hold in Europe back in February and March 2020 I, like others, wondered if this was a time for repentance, for humbling ourselves before God and seeking his mercy. I signed up to a daily prayer bulletin sent out by Christian Media & Arts Australia: COVID19 Call to Prayer. The idea was that collectively we would set aside 19 minutes at 19:00 hours each day to pray.

I found that daily time of prayer to be a blessing during the three-month lockdown that followed in Scotland, where I live with my wife and our children. A time each day to turn our thoughts to God, to focus on the needs of others.

Then the crisis eased, the lockdown was gradually ended, and the prayer bulletin reduced to twice a week. And I stopped praying each evening.

I didn't stop praying completely, I simply reverted to a time of prayer each morning, though even that was often quite rushed and hurried as I prepared for work. I began to long for that daily pause, and wonder if maybe I should step up and provide another guide to daily prayer, and if so, what should that even be about?

At the same time I had been thinking about a goal I set for myself a decade before. I'd accepted a challenge to write 100 goals and before too long, I'd written thirty goals focusing on earning more money, travelling to exotic places, and achieving my career dreams. Then I had a moment of conviction, where was God in all these goals? I decided that I'd better rectify things and wrote my thirty first goal: To be and do all that God wants of me. It struck me at the time that this was potentially a life changing goal, if I really pursued it. Later I decided to name my company after this goal as a constant reminder: Goal 31 Ltd. I had started wondering whether I should use this goal as a theme for my writing, perhaps write a book called The Goal 31 Challenge. I may still do this... Then I began to wonder about inviting people to join me in this challenge, to possibly mentor or disciple them over the course of 31 days. It seemed obvious to me that I would want to pray for them. Which started me thinking about 31 days of prayer...

Since I was already thinking about writing a prayer guide, this seemed a perfect way to do it. 31 days is just a month, right? I could write such a book. People could cope with praying for 31 days. And I wasn't committing myself to something never ending, that would eventually become a burden.

But what should I guide people to pray about? I quickly came back to the theme of repentance, and since I've never seen repentance as a positive experience, I focused in on Jesus first recorded message: "Repent, for the kingdom of heaven is near." Matthew

3 v 2 (NET) The focus on the kingdom of heaven is a positive one. But strangely, what I found as I read about and researched repentance is that it is overwhelmingly positive! Yes, in order to need to repent we have to be distanced from God, there may be sin that needs dealt with, but through every passage I read I found that underneath and behind it all was God's love for us driving the call to repent. God's desire that we be reunited with him, his determination that we not be lost, but find life, and experience this life and the next to the full.

I understood my own need to repent years before I fully grasped God's kindness. One song in particular helped me: Your kindness, by artist Leslie Phillips. Listening to the words of her song I began to understand that God has shown kindness to each one of us, that he wants us to turn back to him, and he enables us to do so. I found that understanding this enabled me to repent, to find forgiveness and peace, to begin a relationship with God.

It might be tempting to view this guide as to be used in the course of one month. After all, there are 31 days in a month. Yet as you'll know, some months have 30 days and February fluctuates... I'd encourage you to just start. Whether on the last day of a month, or the first, or anywhere in between.

I wasn't sure when I started what these 31 days of prayer would end up as. My wife, rather sensibly, told me to finish it before sharing it. It's now been over four months writing and editing. I knew there would be no point trying to share current news to pray over and have opted to share a verse or short passage from the bible each day, some of my own thoughts on repentance and the kingdom of heaven, and a simple prayer. Each day is fairly short, a few pages at most. I offer this to you in the hope it will help. An opportunity to spend thirty-one days reflecting on Jesus first recorded message. I would love to hear whether you found this helpful. You can write to me directly at mark@dragonlake.co.uk

Your challenge, should you choose to accept it, is to spend the next 31 days in prayer.

Yours in Christ

Mark Anderson Smith

Other books by this author

Non-Fiction

The Commands of Jesus

We call Jesus our Lord, we sing praises to him declaring he is our King, yet have we ever fully studied what our King has commanded us to do? We say God is love, God is merciful, God is kind, yet when reading the bible, we find many examples of God commanding his people, and Jesus continuing to do the same to his disciples.

Following on from 31 Days of Prayer, this 31 day study and devotional guide will help you to understand that the commands we are to follow are not simply burdens and drudgery to obey, but a pathway to a more content life, one where we are brought closer to our heavenly father's presence and will be better able to live our lives in peace and in good will with those around us.

The commands of Jesus are a challenge and a blessing and will give you a deeper understanding of Jesus call on your life.

Double Your Salary
…without losing your soul!

An account of one man's attempt to transform his life, placing God first, and seeking to grow and learn in order to provide for his family.

Mark Anderson Smith had what he thought was a well-paid job, until he couldn't afford to buy his children new shoes. That experience made him examine his life and led him to set a goal to double his salary in four years. At the same time he set two other goals to achieve ambitions held since childhood: to gain a university degree, and complete a novel.

He found that working on all three goals at the same time produced a harmonic effect, that making progress towards each goal made the other goals easier to achieve, and allowed him to achieve all three goals in those four years.

Double Your Salary …without losing your soul! offers a balanced perspective on the relationship between the urgency of providing for our needs, with the necessity of making time for family, friends, and faith.

Filled with prompts and suggestions to get you thinking about your own future, encouraging you to set goals and to develop a plan that could transform your life.

There is a common belief that only governments can reduce poverty. Double Your Salary offers you an alternative: you can take control of your career, your future, your life!

Fiction

Fallen Warriors

In the city of York, a young nurse dies in a tragic accident but is mysteriously brought back to life. As she attempts to find out and understand what happened, a group of ordinary people find themselves drawn together: a homeless man tormented by his past, a thief who has crossed a dangerous line, a young Muslim girl searching for answers, a detective hiding a secret, a woman who wants to remove the pastor of her church. Unknown to any of them, an Islamic group secretly plots to form a new Caliphate in the centre of England. York becomes the battle ground for the largest terrorist attack ever faced in the West. Fallen warriors are called to stand and fight, but will they stand or will they fall?

The Great Scottish Land Grab

When his wife is threatened while on a walking holiday in the Scottish Highlands, Robert Castle tries to get justice, only to find the people of Scotland have little rights on their historic land.

Meanwhile, Scotland is preparing to vote on independence when the deaths of senior members of the Scottish Government forces an election.

Disillusioned by his research into Scotland's history, and sensing that the theft of Scotland's land over many centuries has robbed the people of their opportunity to be independent, Castle establishes a new political party and fights for a modern day land grab - to reverse the clearances and return the land that was stolen from Scotland's people.

Challenging an out of touch parliament, Robert turns government on its head by introducing Cafe Politics - a way for communities to debate and agree their own policies.

But how far will Robert go in his determination to overturn the injustice of the Highland Clearances and will he lead Scotland to a better future or into civil war?

About the Author

Mark Anderson Smith is a Scottish author who lived in York for many years and also worked in Tajikistan in Central Asia. Married with three children, he works as an IT Consultant, though aims one day to be able to write full time.

He is the author of two novels including the Christian thriller: Fallen Warriors. He has also written and published an autobiography: Double Your Salary ...without losing your soul! to share what he has learned while building a career and encourage others to lift themselves out of poverty.

Mark is passionate about goals, having seen what a dramatic effect it can have when goals are set that build on each other. A few years ago he accepted a challenge to write down 100 goals. To date he still hasn't stood on a new planet or learned to fly, but insists there is still time. His thirty first goal was the inspiration for his company: Goal 31 Ltd, and in many ways for this book: "To be and do all that God wants of me."

Sign up for Mark's mailing list at:
www.dragonlake.co.uk

Printed in Great Britain
by Amazon